# How I Wrote *2 eBooks* in 21 Days

## Damn Funny. Seriously.

By Glen Stanford

# How I Wrote an ~~an~~ 2
# e-Book in 21 Days

## Damn funny.
## Seriously.

By Glen Stanford

## LARGE PRINT EDITION

(So my Dad can read it.)

# Copyright

Isn't it ironic that the copyright page is usually a cut-and-pasted boilerplate?

How I Wrote 2 eBooks in 21 Days
Damn Funny. Seriously.
Copyright © 2013 by Glen Stanford

Cover illustration by John Cole; inquiries regarding John's illustration and cartoon work can be made via h20vale@msn.com.

Published by Stanford & Stanford Publishing, Naples, Florida

ISBN: 978-0-9889819-2-8

## Disclaimer

# Contents

## Introduction

What's it like to write your first e-book? Is it difficult? Can I do it? Why is there air?

These are all good questions, and I'll tackle most of them here.

We have air because the gravitational pull of the earth holds the oxygen molecules close to the ground into what we have labeled an "atmosphere."

In other words, the earth sucks.

I'm really hoping that my book won't.

I read Steve Scott's *How to Write a Nonfiction eBook in 21 Days*, and it got me enthused enough to write the "how to make money in innkeeping" book that has been bottled up inside of me for two decades. I did indeed make Steve's deadline and completed both *this book* and *THE BREAD IS IN THE BED* exactly

21 days after I put the first note on the first index card.

The day after I decided to write <u>BREAD BED</u>, I thought it might be fun to take notes on the experience. Hey, I'm a rookie; this is my first book. Someday I may want to reminisce about the start of my glory years.

By the end of the third day, I had decided to write *TWO* e-books in 21 days. (Every guy knows that *more is always better*; it's a Y-chromosome thing.) One e-book would be the book about innkeeping, and the second would be *the book about writing the book* about innkeeping. Never one to do things by halves, I have a tendency to bite off more than I can chew (though I will never admit that to my wife).

For example, my lovely bride (everybody say "hi" to Ann. "*Hi, Ann.*") wanted to go sailing, so I signed us up for a 1,500 mile/11 day offshore crewing "opportunity" on a 40ft sailboat traveling from Virginia to the British Virgin Islands. She thought we could use a little exercise, so I arranged for us to hike 650 miles on the Appalachian Trail. She said that I could indulge my whim to look into beekeeping, so I bought *sixteen hives.* You're beginning to get the idea, right? Welcome to my wife's Hell.

The week of January 27 started out much like every other week here in sunny Florida. The skies were clear, the temperature was in the mid-70s; in short: a lot of the "what's not to like" department. That is, until I had the brainstorm to write an e-book. So: sunny outside, brainstorm inside. Are you with me so far? Try to keep up.

"Just do it" the Nike commercials keep telling me. So on that delightfully sunny afternoon on what will hereinafter ever be known as DAY ONE, Monday, January 28, 2013, a day that will most likely not live in too much infamy, I finished Steve's how-to book and decided "Why the heck not?" Pretty inspiring, right?

It was Steve's book that was the last straw on the camel's back (when was the last time you saw a straw laden camel?) It fired-up the final neuron in my brain that said "*You've been gabbing about writing this book for twenty years and it's about time you got off your fat ass and wrote that book; or more to the point, set your fat ass down on a chair and wrote that book.*" It was a pretty big neuron.

This book is the companion piece to _THE BREAD IS IN THE BED_ – a "making-of story" much in the same vein as the making of *Star Wars* films. But with fewer Wookies. It's a behind the scenes look at an ex-innkeeper/ ex-Appalachian Trail hiker /ex-New England Patriots cheerleader/ would-be author and current yacht captain as I try to follow the plan in Steve's book to produce my e-book(s) in 21 days. What makes this book extraordinary is that it is jam-packed with *dozens* of attempts at humor!

It is "blog-like," although the final product is cleaned up and the swear words are edited. I take to heart author John Locke's excellent advice in _How I Sold 1 Million eBooks in 5 Months_. He says that your e-book (and I'm paraphrasing here) can pretty much suck as long as you sell it cheap and a few people like it.

In other words, to be successful with an e-book, you need to find a loyal group of people who enjoy your writing style and would consume anything that you publish. Well, since I devour everything Mr. Locke writes, I can certainly buy into that approach! Plus, he was kind enough to put his picture on the cover so I know when not to open the door.

So, I'm trying to write a whimsical book (make that *TWO* books) with my sense of humor. Not everyone will think that they are knee-slappers, but with any luck there are folks out there who would enjoy them enough to consider telling a friend to *read this dude*. That's me. The dude. Pretty hip, right?

## Day 1 – I've Got a Great Idea

It is Monday, January 28, the heretofore noted day of almost infamy. I called Ann and uttered the words that have been striking fear in her heart since 1982. I said, "*I've got a great idea!*"

I can only imagine what happens to her physiologically speaking when I utter that phrase. Since I was a biology major in college (Washington and Lee University in Lexington, Virginia) I have an educated guess and am going with adrenaline spike, rapid breathing, palm sweating and eye rolling.

I tell her that *we* are finally writing "the innkeeping book" that we have been talking about for years. I can just about hear the gears in her head calculating how much this is going to cost her (my wild schemes tend to give her brain freeze). I can almost hear her pulse rate slow as she comes to the conclusion that at least it won't be too expensive this time.

I make a mental note to keep my brilliant-beyond-brilliant ideas about marketing these e-books to myself. Thirty years of marriage has made me a wiser man.

I tell Ann all about Steve's _21 Days_ book (Steve and I are on a first name basis now, and I'll tell him that if I ever meet him) and that I have been getting writer's cramp filling out index cards for five hours. I tell Ann that she is the de facto co-author of this wonderful enterprise and sense her pulse start to quicken again, and not in that good way.

But she knows how these things go - it's not her first rodeo. This is not the hill she wants to die on, and she (somewhat less than enthusiastically, if you ask me) agrees to join the project. That girl can convey a "Whatever you say, dear" without saying a word.

I'm getting _writer's cramp_ and it's only the first day. I can't wait to get _typer's cramp_. I'm guessing that will quickly lead to _whiner's cramp_, so I do a little bit of research and decide that voice-to-text software might ease all this cramping. I do a quick Google search and order some Dragon software ($51) from Amazon. I am certain that Ann expected that I would be spending *some* money anyway, right? Right? I'm looking for a little support here.

Steve's _21 Days_ book suggests that your project be accomplished in phases. The first phase is the brain dump where, for the first five days, your thoughts erupt haphazardly to index cards. The organization will come later. Then the creative "rough draft" phase for four days where you begin to order your thoughts but don't pay strict attention to sentence structure (or even typos). Then you take a break on Day 9 to work on mechanical items like working with a cover designer. Day 10 starts the paragraph crafting and polishing as you continue refining the work.

So far I can attest to the effectiveness of the brain dump portion of Steve's book. This is brilliant advice and worth the price of admission. I'm getting a continuous flow of thoughts out in a short period of time because I'm not pausing to craft sentences. I'm just firing thoughts to index cards with the plan to organize them later. In the back of my mind, as I'm hoping that all this scribbling will come together, I remember the old joke about the optimistic child flinging manure all around the stable: "*With all this poop, there's got to be a pony in here somewhere!*"

I am taking four Adult Education classes at the local high school. For no reason other than it was the most interesting sounding class offered on Mondays, I signed up for a self-publishing course. (Football season is over, leaving an aching void in my life.) One idea that I had in the back of my mind was to put together an illustrated cookbook since I am a chef and have been photographing my food for years. I had no idea that this course would unlock my long-retired inner innkeeper. Who let that dog out?

Everyone was asked about the book that they were producing. There are about a dozen people in the class, all of whom are either published or soon-to-be published authors as best I can tell. I think I might have been the only one who ever showed up at a publishing class with no intention of actually publishing a book.

The instructor, Lisa Wroble, has been self-publishing for years and has authored 27 books. She made it clear that self-publishing an e-book is not rocket science and anyone can do it. Even if you don't do the formatting and uploading yourself, you can have it done *inexpensively*. Music to Ann's ears.

I had been daydreaming in class about a possible fiction story that I might put together when the innkeeping book idea came out of nowhere and smacked me on the back of the head. Ann was going to be in Boston with her Mom for three weeks and the timing was too much of a coincidence. I was convinced that the Universe was talking to me. Ann is out of town for 21 days – Steve's *21 Day* book; 24 hours in a day – 24 beers in a case? Coincidence? I don't think so.

I purchased Steve's e-book because his title caught my eye; I'm all for getting things done quickly. So between Lisa, Steve, the Universe and fifteen years of innkeeping, I believed it was all fated to come together. I decided right then and there that I would *finally* write the innkeeping book. I got home from class at about 9 o'clock and brain dumped until 4 AM to the index cards that were jumbled around the (tiny, tiny) dent in the mattress where Ann usually slept. I ended up with 75 index cards and a headache. The rest is history.

Well, of course it's *history*; it happened *in the past*. Don't you love it when someone says here's a picture of me when I was younger? *Every picture* of you was taken when you were *younger*.

## Day 2

What a difference a day makes! Ann is a fountain of ideas and enthusiasm! I guess that this innkeeping book has been bottled up inside of her, too. Of course, every innkeeper that we know jokes about writing "the book" someday. We always said the same thing. But with Ann in Massachusetts and me in Florida, I had a stretch of lonely time that was crying out to be filled. Since golfing is infinitely more frustrating than writers block, the book wins.

As a first time book author, I'm thinking that I need to come up with a title before I start doing the serious writing. I want to put the cart and the horse in the proper order. That gets me to thinking about which part of the horse's anatomy you see while sitting on the cart, and I realize that I might be focusing my energies in the wrong direction.

I buy a few marketing e-books that tell me I need a domain name to help my advertising efforts. The horse is definitely pushing the cart now as I buy a domain name for the yet-to-be-written book.

We already have a GoDaddy account for our yacht crewing business (2crew.com), so it was no big deal to add another domain name. They are having a promotion, so I invest $1 to own thebreadisinthebed.com for a year. It sounds like a bargain to me, and I don't want anybody scooping up the name. Yeah, right. As if.

Possible title: Is there a book inside you? I'm not as thrilled with the actual title as I am with the accompanying visual of a guy standing behind an old timey x-ray machine showing a glowing book on the screen. Hey, maybe a beautiful woman behind the x-ray machine with just a hint of nudity. Sex sells, right? I'll tell Ann about her photo op at a more appropriate time.

I went to a cool website (fiverr.com) to order a cover for my e-book. The name tells you everything: it's all kinds of products and services that you can get for five dollars. If I am going to invest five whole bucks in the cover of my book, I had better get my money's worth!

They say that if you want something done; give the job to a busy person. I was hoping a *corollary* would apply, that is, if I forced myself to *be* the busy person, then I would get the jobs done. That was my fuzzy logic, along the lines of *"two wrongs don't make a right, but three rights make a left."* We science majors adore big words like *corollary*. We also enjoy geeky jokes like: "If you are not part of the solution, you're part of the precipitate."

My business e-books also tell me that I should use carefully selected *keywords* in my book title. Google AdWords reports the average number of times a specific word or phrase is searched on Google each month. If I want BREAD BED to rise to the top of the search results pages, I should consider using these terms:

Innkeeping - garners 2k (thousand) searches (or "hits") per month

Inn business – 27k

Best bed breakfast – 40k

Bedandbreakfast (one word) – 74k

Innkeeper – 90k

B and Bs - 2M (million) searches per month - now we're getting somewhere!

How to make money – 5M

Bed breakfast – 9M

B&B – a monstrous 16 Million hits/month

I decide that the whimsical title of my book will be: _THE BREAD IS IN THE BED_. The keyword laden subtitle will be: _How to Make Money as a B&B Innkeeper._ What is the best way to take these most popular searches and cram them into a title without it sounding like a keyword list? Come Hell or high water, the terms "make money" and "B&B" were going to find their way to the cover! The other terms would be included as behind-the-scenes _keywords_.

Incidentally, "Glen Stanford" is searched 320 times per month on Google, and "Dave Barry" is searched 49,500 times per month. That gap is not likely to narrow any time soon. There must be several other _Glen Stanford's_ out there, because I don't Google my name more than 250 times a month. Does it sound indecent when I say that I Google myself?

I put up a blurb on my Facebook page asking if any friends have editorial skills and would like to help. Here's the post:

---

## I'M WRITING A BOOK -- HELP!!!

Calling all editors (or anyone who wants a free shot to punch me in the nose - literally. I mean figuratively. I mean the one where my nose doesn't hurt, but I get free writing advice).

I read an eBook on how to publish an eBook in 21 days. Yeah, right -- 3 weeks -- sure. Nevertheless, it has pushed me over the writing cliff and I'm finally going to do it.

Ann is in Massachusetts with her Mom and I'm here in Florida with my Dad, so the dining room table is free and clear to "brain dump" our soon-to-be best seller on the growing index card pile. Ann gets to brainstorm with me from afar, which is turning out to be the safest place.

Oh, right, the book.

Has to do with innkeeping.

Well duh, right? I mean Ann & I did keep an inn for 15 years and we must have learned SOMETHING!

We figured that there are PLENTY of books that tell innkeepers how to fold napkins and arrange flowers, but not enough (any?) that tell the real behind the scenes horror (first edit, make that "challenges") associated with actually making MONEY.

We're ready to let out the secret tricks of the trade. OK, maybe not secrets, but the things that worked (or flopped) for us over 15 years. And to talk about the unspeakable horror (there's that word creeping back in again) of trying to make a buck in the keeping of an inn.

So, we need a snappy title.

As of now, the working title (and subtitle) are:

The Bread Is In The Bed

(How to make money as B&B Innkeepers)

If you have any editing skills, we need eyes. Hell, even if you don't have skills and just want a free "almost book" and a thank you on our Acknowledgement page, let us know and we'll send you a copy.

OK, an actual copy of an actual manuscript is a gleam in our eyes now. But if we're to stick to the 21 day plan, we need to send you the draft by TUESDAY, FEBRUARY 12.

And here is the important part -- YOU have to read it and get your notes/comments/nose punches back to us BY FEBRUARY 16 (and the sooner the better!)

That's not a lot of time, but time is money and money is the root of all evil and evil is bad and bad is not good and so time is good. What are you wasting time for? Send us an email if you want to help. We'll send you the Microsoft Word "almost book" on Feb 12.

Free nose punches. Promise I won't get mad. This time.

Send your help offer to our email: glenann@2crew.com

Thanks friends!

## Day 3

It occurred to me sometime during the night that it might be fun to *write a book about writing my first book*, and that I should take notes as I write BREAD BED. You're probably getting a sense of how I think by now, so you won't be surprised if I decide to not stop there, would you? Why not make a visual record to go along with the blog? So I get out my camera, put it on the tripod and start snapping photos of the index card explosion on the dining room table. I successfully combat the urge to take a video of me taking photos of my writing the book about writing the book. Now that would just be silly. Who says I don't have willpower?

I also decide that I don't want this book to be the poor sister to *THE BREAD IS IN THE BED*. Lady Mary gets all the attention and Lady Edith is always ignored. What, everyone doesn't watch Downton Abbey?

I will do the same steps for *this book* that I do on BREAD BED. I'll do the market research on keywords and spend another five bucks on a cover. I love all my aristocratic Crawley sisters the same.

I call Ann and say, "*I have great idea*!" You know the drill: heart, respiration, palms, and eyes. "*What is it this time*," she asks through what sounds like a forced smile. I tell her my idea about *writing a book about writing the book* expecting a Whiskey Tango Foxtrot, but she takes it in stride. Her math is getting quicker.

11:56 AM - I have the bright idea to start putting times into *the book within a book*. Who knows if these time stamps will make it into the final version, but I will have them for my own enjoyment. At this point I need to try to remember *exactly* what happened in the last two days. So I start making more notes on index cards while I enjoy a wonderful bowl of chili for lunch.

Possible book title: *The Best Cup of Coffee You'll Ever Spend*

1:18 PM - The chili is talking to me, saying, *"Boy I sure was delicious, but maybe you shouldn't have added so much hot sauce."* I realize that it would be prudent to leave a stack of index cards and a pen on the bathroom counter.

6:07 PM - I have the 3-taco special at Taco Bell. I have never written a blog before, but I understand that details like this are important.

6:30 PM – It's Wednesday night at Adult Ed, and that means it's Bluegrass Class – my favorite night of the week. We take turns leading the class with songs, and mine are: *The Wreck of the Old 97* (which is indeed a train wreck when I lead it) and *Man of Constant Sorrow* from the movie <u>O Brother, Where Art Thou</u>. On my way to class I bought a costume beard at the local party store, and when I got up for *Man of Constant Sorrow*, I did my best George Clooney impersonation in the shaggy gray beard. We were all laughing so hard it was hard to keep time with the music. Joe recorded the song with his phone camera, and who knows, by now we are all probably YouTube sensations. I've been too busy to check, but Leno hasn't called yet.

I've received all sorts of Facebook responses, including memories of fun stuff, things not to forget in the book, and volunteers for editing. My original intention of putting this on FB was to "put it out there" so I couldn't chicken out on the project. To burn the bridge behind me so I would *have* to move forward and write the book. I got quite the bonus tear in my eye from my friends offering all kinds of encouragement. Sniff.

Apropos of nothing, the world's best knock knock joke:

Knock, knock!
Who's there?
Control freak - now you say "control freak who?"

1:02 AM - I am hitting the hay happy - the index cards are on the table like little ducks in a row. And like the duck that flew upside down, I think I'm quacking up. Okay, maybe I'm a little punchy, too.

## DAY 4 – National Procrastination Day

This will be the only day that I bore you with the minutiae of the day. But looking back on my daily notes really tickled my Elmo.

7:32 AM - Rise and shine! I can't sleep with all these thoughts exploding in my alleged brain. I'm going to have to make a master to-do list to organize this nonsense.

But priorities must come first, so I Google *"Rise and Shine"* and learn that it was a 1990 Steppenwolf album that brought us that snappy tune *"We Like It, We Love It (We Want More of It)."*

Miscellaneous thoughts kept coming to me in the middle of the night. With each stray thought I had to force myself to open one eye to write it down. Now it is morning and I need to incorporate these cards into the growing dining room table piles arranged by subject. I've also got two appointments today, one with a painter and one with Comcast, so I'll need to schedule writing around real world intrusions.

Unrelated joke and the second of many lost and ludicrous thoughts of the day: Why don't Quakers believe in pre-marital sex? It could lead to dancing!

One card reminds me that I have to call Luiz the computer guy to help me put together the web page. I want to have content available on thebreadisinthebed.com that will be bonus information for this book (The daily photographs immortalizing the messy process can be seen there.)

I come up with the structure of *THE BREAD IS IN THE BED*. I'm going to write it in two parts: *before you buy* the inn and *after you're stuck*. These are two different sets of advice that logically fall into these categories. I won't bore you with them here, you can invest another cup of coffee into that book if you want the ghastly details.

I still don't have a working title for this book. Now I am just calling it *BOOK TWO*. I want it to be whimsical; something like "*How I Wrote An e-Book in 21 Days*," with the word "Wrote" scribbled out and a carat between the words "I" and "Wrote" pointing to the new words "Didn't Write." Too pessimistic?

These are the things that hit me in the middle of the night, and I didn't get to sleep until Chinese dentist. That's tooth-hurty (2:30) in the morning. Yes, I get punchy and politically incorrect after midnight…

8:00 AM – I fired up the laptop and logged on to Facebook only to see that someone complained to them that I sent a friend request to someone I didn't know. My first thought was "isn't that what Facebook is all about, making new friends?" But then I thought *wait a minute*, I rarely send out friend requests! I had to promise Facebook that I understood the Friending Policy before they would let me see my page.

What irks me is that I have sent out a grand total of *two* Facebook friend requests in the last three months, and now the Friend Police are on my doorstep. My Aunt Edie was kind enough to accept a friend request back in December, so I don't think she was the one who ratted me out. The other was a friend request I sent out *yesterday afternoon* to an author friend of a friend. My friend Wendy said that this author friend of hers was very knowledgeable and would be a great resource if I needed assistance.

Some resource; she turns me into the Friend Police for bugging her. Are these my new peeps - prissy authors with time enough on their hands to narc to the Facebook constabulary? Writers' conventions must not be very fun.

8:15 AM – The painter arrives so I don't have time to stew over friends, real or imagined. Our condo association is painting the exteriors of all the buildings and they need to send painters through each unit to paint the lanais (that's screened porches for those of you who don't speak Floridian).

10:17 AM - Well, life seems to be getting in the way this morning. I have the painter here; the Comcast guy is coming sometime between 1PM and July, and I have to work on some boat stuff.

Our real job is serving as Captain and Mate on boats owned by a wonderful family in New Hampshire. Winter is for coordinating with boat yards, and summer is for enjoyable sailing around New England. I am contemplating these happier times as I look out the window and watch the painter work.

The index cards are organized into cheerful little rows, and I feel as if I am ahead of schedule so I have a nice chat with Richard the painter.

Clearly I had Vermont innkeeping on the brain and I told Richard about the summer we had the whole inn painted by Appalachian Trail thru-hikers. It's a fun story. Starting on April fool's day in 2000, we hiked for six weeks from Springer Mountain (in Georgia, the start of the trail) to Virginia. We met quite a few hikers that were trying to hike the entire 2,180 miles to Maine, and they would be coming within 5 miles or so of the inn.

We told our hiking friends that if they looked us up when they got to Vermont, we would house them and feed them beer. All they would have to do is give us a couple of hours of painting. By the time July rolled around, hikers started to knock on our door. The story had grown on the trail (as these things do) and the inn became, shall we say, quite popular. It must have been the enticement of free beer since you get pretty thirsty after 1,700 trail miles!

Well, we didn't just fall off the turnip truck. When you have a parade of willing (if not stinky) friends that want to help you paint, you let them! I made more trips to the True Value hardware store that summer than in the other fourteen years combined. Anything that didn't move got painted. The dog must have been napping that day. We changed her name to Spot. Anyway, I'm pretty sure Richard was eyeing the door by the time I got to the end of the story. At this point the astute reader will begin to sense that there is a little procrastination going on.

10:59 AM - I decide that the poinsettias need watering. Of course, it's the first time that I have watered them in a month. Procrastination alert! It's not that I feel overwhelmed (okay maybe a little) it's just that I'm thinking that I only have to organize the index cards today. I don't have to do any actual writing until tomorrow. And they're already in those neat little rows. Heaven forbid I get ahead of the game.

11:02 AM - I have a brilliant-beyond-brilliant brainstorm, which of course does not include doing any writing on the book. I think I'll have a section on the webpage called "the cutting room floor." I can include tidbits that don't quite make it into the book. I really only want BREAD BED to focus on the money making aspects of innkeeping. There are dozens of ideas that innkeepers know (collectively, anyway) and if I included all of them it would start to look like many other innkeeping "how-to" books.

It is my intention to sell this book "dirt cheap." Actually, I'm going to sell it cheaper than dirt. I (having of course nothing else to do today) Googled *Home Depot* to check on the price of a bag of dirt. You can invest $22.97 in the *"Premium Professional Mix with Fertilizer,"* which I think is a good comparison because I am also including fertilizer. You could buy both of my books and still have plenty of money left to pot a dozen plants.

11:17 AM - I'm going nowhere fast. This is turning into what Appalachian Trail thru-hikers call a "zero day." There is a saying on the trail, *"You've got to hike in the rain if you want to get to Maine."* Now I'm getting the writer's equivalent of "town gravity" where you can't pull yourself out of a nice hotel room to climb up the wet hill to keep slogging down the trail. (All trail towns are in valleys, so you always have to get psyched to hike up and out of towns.)

11:30 AM - I've been up since 7:30 AM and running on coffee (whoops). I think I'll pop lunch into the microwave (oh, how the mighty have fallen) and attack the writing after I eat.

I decide to nuke some pulled pork from Omaha Steaks. I guess I didn't really learn yesterday's chili lesson. I'm toasting a bun because, well, it takes longer. I decide to document this lunch with a few photographs. Exciting bonus - see thebereadisinthebed.com for a photograph of the sandwich that I ate at 11:38 AM on January 31, 2013. Maybe I'll put in a photo of me *after* I ate it (using free artwork of a guy with great abs and a disclaimer that these are not the author's actual abs). Don't like my sense of humor? You can join Ann's support group.

11:38 AM - Comcast is running ahead of schedule and they'll be here in twenty minutes. Great - now I won't be interrupted this afternoon (he says to himself knowing it justifies twenty more minutes to empty the dishwasher, refill the Keurig and sweep the kitchen floor). I mean, why start into a stack of index cards when I'm only going to be interrupted? That little voice in the back of my brain tells me I'm procrastinating again (shut up shut up shut up).

11:55 AM - As I am famously known as a strong-willed individual, I successfully resist the urge to alphabetize the glassware. I mean, that would just waste valuable time. Probably. Do coffee cups go before glasses because "c" comes before "g?" Or are coffee cups actually "mugs" and should therefore be filed under "m" on the starboard side of the shelf? Note to self: do a Google search to see what everyone else is doing. It will save precious time.

11:57 AM - Last thoughts on this incredibly unproductive morning. Will this book tell you how to write a book? Will this book tell you how to improve your prose? Will this book help you find ideas to write about? Heck no! But it *will* show that you can still write an e-book in 21 days even if you're not devoting *all of your waking minutes* to the writing.

12:00 PM - And so begins the afternoon. We're off like a herd of turtles. Note to self - research what God did on day four and see if I'm ahead of Her.

12:02 PM - I decide that I like writing e-books so much that my next books will come out two at a time: the book that I am writing and the writing of the book that I am writing. Of course, it's easy to be confident when you haven't written a damn thing yet!

12:08 PM - I have a nice chat with Will, the Comcast guy. Our cable box has had some challenges lately, so I called for service. This was before I decided to write a book (*way* back, four days ago).

Great news! We are getting a storage upgrade from 160 to 500 gigs on the new Comcast box! I knew you'd be as excited as I am. Plus, I don't see how this could *possibly* be a distraction to my writing.

I tell Will that I'm writing a book about writing a book, and that he's now starring in the procrastination section. He tells me that I'm "*meta*," meaning *the game within the game*. I thought briefly about putting the word "*meta*" in the title, but that would probably leave me wide open for bad reviewer puns (as in, "I never *meta* book I didn't like until this one.")

By now Will has the new cable box installed and we're waiting for it to boot. He calls this the "Six longest minutes in the universe." If he only knew.

Will catches a glimpse into the second bedroom that is set up as a writing area and home recording studio. So far this room has seen bad prose and worse bluegrass.

Will studied professional recording (as in music and sound systems) in college. He worked on a cruise ship in the sound department for the entertainers. He said that there were 900 crew members on his ship, and what was remarkable to him was that all nationalities worked very well together with no fighting. This reminds me to put a note in BREAD BED that says if you have a prejudiced bone in your body, don't even consider innkeeping.

I tell Will that I am a yacht captain with both American and British licenses, but that I need to get sea time on larger ships so that I can increase my license tonnage. He tells me what I already know, that there are British and Italian crews on many of these ships. In fact, he has never met an American working on a ship's bridge. I explained that Americans don't traditionally train for careers as boat crew unlike the Brits, Italians and the South Africans. Plus we have a bad reputation in the industry for being sue happy. This reminds me: *I am not liable for permanent damage to your funny bone beyond the price of this book.*

Just when Will begins to see that those six minutes can be a *really* long time, the cable box boots and he's free to go. If I'm not careful, I'll get a bad reputation for talking the ear off of these service guys.

12:39 PM – I shake hands with Will and tell him to look for his name in the book on February 20. I couldn't possibly miss any deadlines, right?

12:48 PM - Comcast calls me with a customer satisfaction survey. I feel that I owe Will a good review since he was kind enough to put up with my blathering. He gets top ratings across the board, and I even left the optional voice message telling Comcast that "Will was highly knowledgeable, very helpful and a nice guy to boot. You're lucky to have him." Another 2 1/2 minutes bites the dust.

12:50 PM - Back to work. But first, a quick bathroom break.

1:00 PM - Okay, *now* back to work. But wait, I've got to call the boatyard in Maine to go over a few things. I'm sure that I mentioned that Ann and I work on yachts. Boy have we got some sea stories! Do you know the difference between a fairytale and a sea story? A fairytale starts with "Once upon a time;" a sea story starts with "you are not going to f-ing believe this."

But that's the subject for another book (or two).

1:41 PM - Well I guess it's pretty clear which book is getting the most attention today. Plus I had to make sure that the cable was working, so I watched the end of the movie *The Day After Tomorrow*. I really do like Dennis Quaid and it made me think of one of my all-time favorite movies, *The Parent Trap*. I really miss Natasha Richardson; and Lindsay, you were a delightful 12-year-old actor. I even liked you in *Freaky Friday* with Jamie Lee Curtis, who was born the same year as I was. But I digress.

1:53 PM - This just isn't working. I'm going for a walk around the block. I'll take a pen and an index card just in case genius rears its ugly head and I can't keep a thought in my brain for forty whole minutes.

2:37 PM - I'm back from my walk. And it wasn't a total waste of time. I chatted with Ann about the most important trait of an innkeeper. Customer service! What, you were expecting toilet paper folding? Of course customer service as a category is a no-brainer. It's really *how* you do it that counts. There *are* tricks of the trade. But that's the subject of another book (insert shameless plug here for the <u>*THE BREAD IS IN THE BED*</u>).

2:47 PM - My secret weapon has arrived! I'm Ralphie in <u>*A Christmas Story*</u> with my new Red Ryder BB Gun. (*Hope I don't poke my eye out!*) I'm Steve Martin in <u>*The Jerk*</u> when he cries *"The new phone book is here! The new phone book is here!"* I'm little Ronnie Howard in <u>*The Music Man*</u> singing *"The Wells Fargo wagon is a-commin' down the street!"* I'm that little kid on the Disney commercial who is *"Too excited to sleep!"*

HOORAY! - I just received my Dragon speech recognition software that "turns talk into type." Did I mention that I don't know how to type? It's only Day 4 and already I have writer's cramp. If I have to hunt and peck through the keyboard to get this book written I'll be here through next Arbor Day.

4:28 PM - I don't know what I was thinking, but this voice recognition software needs to be trained to your voice (and you need to learn how to use it). What a newbie I am! And no, I am not missing the irony that I am writing one book where I am (*supposedly*) an expert and writing a second book as I struggle up the learning curve.

Just what I needed today: a way to kill some time! Well, at least I got to reuse the cardboard box that the software came in. I boxed up the first four seasons of the Big Bang Theory to send to my friends in New Jersey. I've been promising to do this for about six months and figured this is as good a time as any. By the way, the Big Bang Theory is brilliant.

4:45 PM - I'm off to have dinner with my brother before I go to class tonight. Did I mention that I am taking *four* Adult Ed classes each week? I'll come back later and continue training the Dragon. Does that sound dirty, or is it just me?

On Mondays I have Self-Publishing class. *"Hey, no fair! Flag on the play! I thought you said that you were starting this project from scratch?"* Well, I am. I'll admit that the class got my creative juices boiling, but I didn't actually *decide* to write a book until the evening of the third class (three nights ago). The class taught me that the whole publication process isn't intimidating, so it removed a lot of the unknowns that may have been holding me back. The hard part is *actually writing the book* - everything else is pretty straightforward.

On Tuesdays I have fishing class. Although I work as a yacht captain, fishing is definitely a hole in my resume. I have sailed over 75,000 miles and caught nothing but seaweed. Ann has had better luck, pulling in three yellow fin tuna just outside of Tonga. I'm confident that an adult education class at the local high school will turn me into an expert fisherman in no time.

Wednesday night is Bluegrass night! There are about 25 of us that holler and wail the evening away. I play the guitar and the ukulele. (Is there anything this guy can't do? Yeah, play the guitar and the ukulele.)

Thursday (tonight) is Photoshop class. It's a lot of fun and a easier than going on a diet. I guess the point is, I am writing these books and still trying to keep a semblance of a real life at the same time.

I put a little blurb on my Facebook page asking for editing help from my friends. An old college buddy, Hunt, wrote back and told me that he's an author and believes that I might be a tad unrealistic in my plan to write an e-book in 21 days. Boy, am I glad that I didn't tell him I'm actually trying to write TWO e-books in 21 days.

Hunt tells me that in his experience, nonfiction books are written at about a 750 words/day pace and that I shouldn't get too discouraged if it takes longer than I'm expecting.

I expect that 750 words a day is more of a "finished product" count, and not the "creative first draft" word count that I am going through now. Nevertheless,

Microsoft Word keeps a running tally of the word count, so from now on that will be my last daily entry.

11:57 PM -

*THE BREAD IS IN THE BED* word count - 0

BOOK TWO word count - 3,110 (I guess that counts the words in the word count. How meta.)

## DAY 5

4:25 AM - I set my alarm for 9:30 AM because I am going to dad-sit my 86-year old father today. Wishful thinking on the sleep thing, though. For two hours thoughts keep coming to me so I open one eye to jot them on index cards. At 6:45 I force myself to just shut down and try to get back to sleep. I'm tired of clicking the light on and off. Can I still buy "*The Clapper*" somewhere?

7:13 AM - My next door neighbor decides that this would be the optimal time to hang pictures on the wall, so he's apparently pounding in hooks. Or maybe he's strangling a duck, I don't know. I jot this stray thought down on an index card just in case it's important, pull the covers over my head and try to get some sleep.

7:18 AM - Sunrise. Damn this bedroom window with Eastern exposure. I decide to get out of bed and start the coffee. While it's brewing I count up the index cards: 47 of them last night (31 for BREAD BED, 12 for this book and another 4 for miscellaneous real life items). One of the cards is pretty undecipherable, except for the exclamation points and circled stars around the words "incredibly naïve." I wonder what that meant.

According to the 21 Days schedule, today is the day that I start actually writing the rough draft on *THE BREAD IS IN THE BED*. So I take my coffee over to the computer and start typing. I mean start yakking into the microphone. I'm really starting to like this talk-to-type stuff! Can you get yakker's cramp?

8:15 AM - It's official. My great American novel/business/comedy/innkeeper self-help book is underway. I have put the first 359 words to the page. Oh sure, I still need to add thirty thousand more words and then pound them into coherence, but at least I'm out of the starting gate.

I send a text to Ann asking her to call People's Linen and get the current cost for renting sheets and towels (one of our pieces of advice in BREAD BED is to *rent* linens.) I am clearly much too busy doing important stuff, and these plebeian tasks need to be farmed out to staff (love you, honey!)

I send a quick email to the cover designer to tell him to insert the word "_More_" into the subtitle of _THE BREAD IS IN THE BED_. I tell him to change "_How to Make Money as a B&B Innkeeper_" into "_How to Make More Money as a B&B Innkeeper_" with the word "_More_" written above the line and a ^ pointing up to it so it looks like a last second revision. Art imitates life. I like saying cover designer; it makes me sound like a big time author. Actually, he's some fellow at the other end of fiverr.com who is designing my e-book cover for five bucks. I am clearly a big spender.

9:23 AM - I pack up my ukulele and laptop to head over to dad's house. Dad has "memory challenges," and to pass the time we sing a lot of Kumbaya. And I mean a lot. I really hate that song.

10:56 AM - I'm over at dad's house showing him the talk-to-type software. He says he feels like he's a million years old and that it looks like magic. In his day the boss dictated letters to the secretary who would return an hour later with the transcript. He can't believe his eyes when my words appear instantly on the screen.

Suddenly, I experience a nasty adrenaline spike as it appears that I've somehow lost this morning's work!

There is no time to grieve, however, because dad has a pretty good amount of energy and we are going to take advantage of that and drive to the Gentlemen's Club. The GC is a group of about thirty memory patients who get together every Friday for lunch and good old fashioned camaraderie. We stand for the *Pledge of Allegiance* (hand over hearts, of course) sing *God Bless America* and some other corny songs, re-fight the occasional World War II battle and reminisce about the 1943 Red Sox - you know, the usual stuff that octogenarians gab about.

If we are going to get to Gentlemen's Club in time for lunch, I'll have to get the show on the road. Organizing the dad parade helps me forget my misery over the lost file. In order to get dad out of the house, I have to get him into his walker, over to the stairs, down the stairs, switch air hoses to a portable air cylinder (did I mention that he's on oxygen?) out the door with his outdoor walker (the one with wheels) and trail him with the oxygen tank. Then I have to load this carnival into the car, take the air hose out of his nose, put him in the car, pass the air hose back to him, buckle him in, load up the folding walker, and go back into the house for more Kleenex. I consider this a small sacrifice to be saved from an afternoon of Kumbaya.

3:41 PM - Just got back from Gentlemen's Club. I took a handheld phone video of the gang singing God Bless America. I'll put it on the webpage if you'd like to see it (as if you have nothing better to do). My dad is the one who sings *"bud-ee-up"* after "from the mountains" and after "to the prairies." You can see when I jiggle the camera phone because I was laughing as I caught (Group Leader) Debbie's eye across the room - we always wait for my dad to sing the *"bud-ee-up"* part. Never fails to entertain.

6:03 PM – Great news! I get home and learn that I didn't lose the morning's work after all. I had just saved the file on an external hard drive instead of the laptop. I was using two sources to store the files in case one got corrupted, and I had simply outsmarted myself. That's not hard to do.

I'm ready to resume writing, but my brother Ron is in the neighborhood and has popped by to say hello. He's just learning to play the ukulele, so we play a couple of songs and then I kick him out the door. I taught him Kumbaya. I can be cruel that way.

9:38 PM - I've been going great guns on the manuscript. Finally! Except for a brief visit by Pedro, the Domino's pizza delivery guy, I've been at the keyboard for a few hours. And I didn't even stop to chat with Pedro.

9:57 PM - I find myself tweaking paragraphs and shifting them around. This is supposed to be the creative phase where I just get the words on the computer. I'm not supposed to be working on the second draft until next Wednesday, five days from now. I think I'll take a shower and try to refocus.

10:32 PM - I've got a better idea. I'll re-focus in the morning. I'm going to send the files to Ann and hit the pillow.

_THE BREAD IS IN THE BED_ word count – 1,956
BOOK TWO word count – 4,032

# DAY 6

8:51 AM - I slept great last night! I read an investment newsletter completely unrelated to writing at around 11:30 and drifted off to sleep somewhere around midnight. I didn't wake up until around 8:30 when the next-door neighbor apparently needed to hang the rest of his artwork.

I didn't dream of the writing, nor did I wake up and write a single note card. It's an interesting feeling and my brain feels like it's been rebooted. It's the first Saturday in the three-week write-a-book program, and I have the stray thought that this would also be the first full day that someone with a real mid-week job would be devoting to write his book. I have high hopes for getting in three writing sessions today. My calendar is clear, there is no one in the condo, and except for the occasional duck strangling it's rather peaceful.

I did have one flash of inspiration after yesterday's lost file almost-debacle. I decided that I will email file backups to Ann each night. This way I'll have three copies, one of them in Massachusetts. At least the only files in existence won't be sitting six inches away from each other.

10:27 AM - Just got off the phone with Ann. It was her first look at the drafts. She really loved the stuff, but didn't want us to tell all the good stories right at the beginning. She thought we should save the funny stuff for later in the book. I told her that I am a bottomless fount of fun, frivolity and storytelling. Did you know that you can actually feel someone rolling her eyes over the phone?

She had some great ideas for stories. Brain neurons are firing left and right for both of us now as we remember things that happened to us as far back as (oh, the humanity) 25 years. I would tell you that this girl still gives me plenty of ideas, but I don't want *you* to get the wrong idea.

Suddenly there's more racket from next door. How many ducks does this guy have, anyway? I have always read where authors need to lock themselves away into quiet rooms and not be disturbed. That's why they head for the proverbial cabin in the woods! I don't know how anybody with children could concentrate enough to write a book. Anyway, I called Ann to tell her that I will be "going dark" for a couple of hours so that I can concentrate on the writing. It sounds very secret agent like, but I'm just muting my cell phone. James Bond would be so proud.

12:02 PM - Despite my earlier promise to focus on the creative rough draft I find myself re-reading previous paragraphs and doing minor corrections. (Stop it, stop it, stop it!)

But while I am doing this, I notice that it is being written in two different fonts, which has been making me nuts. I do a little research to find out why this is so, and apparently I have been opening some of these files in two different programs: Microsoft Word and OpenOffice. Mystery solved. I switch both books to New Times Roman Size 10 and head to the kitchen to microwave some lunch.

1:52 PM - Stray thoughts continue to pop into my head and I am STILL writing index cards and filing them on the dining room table. It's like taking Ann to the jewelry store. She sees something shiny and dashes over to the next display case. And after she reads this, I suspect there will be another trip to the jewelry store in my future.

3:10 PM - For the first time I can see this project happening on time! And all I did was put the headings and subheadings on the manuscript. What a difference! It looks so professional! The index card piles on the dining room table no longer seem intimidating. I no longer fear them - it is their turn to fear me. I am an e-book author, hear me roar. Now if I get a stray thought I'll just blurt it into the proper subheading section of the manuscript (instead of to an index card) and attend to it later.

The last thing bothering me is that I haven't put Days 1-3 into *this* manuscript. They are still haphazard index card scribbles since I did not get my voice-to-text software until Day 4.

So I'll take a couple of hours and get *this book* caught up to the moment. But just to confuse you further, you should know that everything that was written before Day 4 was kept on index cards and not blogged until Day 6. Day 4 (and on) are written in "real time." Clear as mud, right?

11:59 PM - It took me all evening to get caught up on the first three days. But from now on I will not have to remember previous days and will be writing only in "real time."

*THE BREAD IS IN THE BED* word count – 4,865
BOOK TWO word count – 9,298

## Day 7

I woke up this morning with a tiny concern nagging at the back of my brain. And you know it has to be a pretty tiny concern if it can hide itself behind my brain.

I was wondering if my book was going to be long enough. How many pages should this be before somebody feels like they've been ripped off for their price of a cup of coffee? I have been reading on Kindles for so long that I've gotten over the page number mindset and now only look at the way Kindle does it: "locations" and "percentage of the way" through the book.

So if I write ten pages on Microsoft Word, how many "locations" is that? I consult Dr. Google and find what seems to be a reasonable answer. Reasonable enough anyway, for me to hogtie that stray thought and toss its little butt kicking and screaming out of the back of my mind. I need all the brain space I can get.

I did a very quick look at the two books that inspired me to write my books, Steve Scott's _How to Write a_

*Nonfiction eBook in 21 days* and John Locke's *How I Sold 1 Million eBooks in 5 Months*. Steve's book has 1,165 "locations," and John's book has 2,851.

One of the popular answers that I found said that Kindle will have approximately 16.69 "locations" per printed book page. So the down and dirty is Steve's e-book has 1,165 locations/16.69 = 70 pages; John's book has 2,851 locations/16.69 = 171 pages.

Another rough cut is that every 1000 words equals *approximately* 4 book pages.

I didn't want to delve too deeply into this; I just wanted a rough idea of how many printed book pages (and "locations") my e-books would have.

I had my answer. I would be satisfied if my book is somewhere between 70 and 171 pages. Microsoft Word not only counts the words, but of course keeps a running tally of pages. As of now, BOOK TWO is 21 pages long and *THE BREAD IS IN THE BED* is 11 pages long. Just when I thought I was making some real headway, I start to feel that I'm at the bottom of Hysteria Hill looking up.

Picture Michelangelo lying on his back at the top of the scaffolding in the Sistine Chapel. His creative genius is flowing, and he's just painted a finger. Is that God's or some guy's finger? Who knows? The point is he's still got to paint the rest of God, throw in a few angels and prophets, maybe a cloud or flying carpet, and definitely a fig leaf for the guy. Michelangelo didn't have time to stop and worry at this early point, and neither do I.

Today I wrote the BREAD BED section on developing repeat business. I'm rather amazed at the well of emotions coming up as I remember people and friends from years past. Although we never lost sight of the inn as being a business venture, you can't help but grow close to some wonderful guests through the years.

Since today is Super Bowl Sunday, I am giving myself permission to knock off for a while and root for the 49ers. Four hours later, there is no joy in Mudville as the 49ers lose Super Bowl XLVII (that's 47 if you don't speak Roman) to the Baltimore Ravens in a heartbreaker. Going to hit the hay and start fresh in the morning.

_THE BREAD IS IN THE BED_ word count – 8,763

BOOK TWO word count – 11,716

## Day 8

I'm starting to get that bad feeling that the day is slipping away from me. I have a Super Bowl hangover and I didn't have even have anything to drink! I woke up at around 8 AM ready to hit the ground running, only to find that real life is rearing its ugly head. First I get a call from the bank looking for more paperwork as we try to refinance our Florida condominium.

Have you ever tried to refinance a Florida condominium? Both words – "Florida" and "condominium" - are swear words to bankers nowadays. When you put them together in the same sentence you can almost hear the bankers running away screaming.

It's Monday, so I'm going to publishing class tonight, and I decide that I will ask the class for some free help. These folks are in the same boat as I am as many are going to publish their first books. I'm thinking that they might get a kick out of this blog book, though I suspect that they're going to think that

I am nuts trying to write two books in three weeks. I'll ask them anyway. Once you are a ukulele player, very little else seems to embarrass you.

It is only Day 8, but I have already written in the manuscript these words: *"I did indeed make Steve's deadline, and finished BREAD BED exactly 21 days after I put the first note in the first index card."* I'm not sure if this sentence will make it to the final version, but I have decided that I will honor the spirit of it. Innkeeping stories keep coming to me in a seemingly endless parade, and guests, fellow innkeepers and former chambermaids have already found out about the book (from my Facebook post) and are making story suggestions.

I suspect that there will be even more story suggestions as previous guests come across this book. I hope to hear from them, and maybe they can remind me of more stories that I have buried deep inside my brain. So as of now (Mr. Big Talker) I am intending to update BED BREAD with additional stories as they become available, therefore I might as well draw the line somewhere and tidy up the book on Day 21. Otherwise, I could be forever adding stories.

Plus, I'm already envisioning the words *"New and Improved"* on the cover. Is it just me, or does "new and improved" not make sense to you either? Isn't something either new *or* improved? How can it be *both*?

11:47 AM - Huge news! Incredible news! Wonderful news! Ann's mom is in remission!

The whole reason that Ann and I are separated this month is that she has been with her mother while her mom gets chemotherapy in the Boston area. I am staying with my dad because we're getting near the tail end of his ability to remember things, and I am dreading the day that he doesn't recognize me when I walk into the room. It's moments like this that make me realize just how precious life is and that we need to cherish our loved ones while we still can.

I'd like to think it's a testament to my good nature because it takes a whole minute for the penny to drop. While I'm smiling so wide my cheeks start to ache, light dawns on Marble Head that this turn of events is going to throw a wrench (a wonderful wrench yes, but still a wrench) into my plan to write TWO e-books in 21 days.

It means that Ann's mom will not be undergoing chemotherapy treatments for the next few weeks, and that they can come down to Florida! Ann is looking at the JetBlue webpage right now to see how soon they can get here.

As I have temporarily converted the second bedroom into my writing studio, I'm going to have to do a quick reshuffle to get the room ready for my mother-in-law. I know what *my mom* would have said about my instantly transforming the second bedroom into a writing studio: "Would you jump in my grave that fast?" The funny gene comes from mom's side; we always had to explain the jokes to dad.

Don't get me wrong, I'm thrilled that Ann and her mom are coming down here. But it remains to be seen just how much I can concentrate with two ladies under the roof for the last nine days of the project.

I brought the first page of each book to publishing class tonight. When class was over, I stood up and told everybody that I had some free scratch paper for them, and on the other side was the first page to the two books I was writing in 21 days. I could tell that Lisa was thinking that I was making the typical rookie mistake trying to publish too soon (and I can't say that I necessarily disagree with her!). I was pleasantly surprised when everyone in class was kind enough to take my hand out and not immediately crumple it for the circular file. As I walked with my classmate Katrina after class, she was sure that I had a bestseller on my hands. Who wouldn't want to read a comedy about someone trying to write two books in three weeks? My readership fan base is growing by leaps and bounds, now totaling three people.

According to the 21 Day plan, tomorrow is the day that I need to finish the rough draft. There is still an appreciable pile of index cards on the dining room table, and innkeeping stories keep popping into my head or arriving from friends in my email and on Facebook.

I'm satisfied that I am remembering a lot of good stories that illustrate the points I want to convey to prospective innkeepers, but I'm anxious that I won't put them in the perfect order. Of course I will have six days to move the story locations around. I'm telling myself that since I "wasted" time polishing up some paragraphs when I should have been in the creative phase, that I'm *owed* another day or two of rough drafting. Cognitive dissonance at its best.

I have fishing class tomorrow, but I might need to play hooky.

*THE BREAD IS IN THE BED* word count – 12,348
BOOK TWO word count – 12,961

## Day 9

I'm thinking about persistence and how it pays off.

A neuron fires in the back of my brain (I do have more than one you know; neuron, that is, not brain) as I remember the graduation speech that I gave as Class President at Wm. Fremd H.S. in Palatine, Illinois. Part of my speech included the inspirational poem: *DON'T QUIT* (author unknown). The first stanza is as follows:

> When things go wrong, as they sometimes will,
> When the road you're trudging seems all uphill,
> When the funds are low and the debts are high,
> And you want to smile, but you have to sigh,
> When care is pressing you down a bit,
> Rest, if you must, but don't you quit.

I read *all four stanzas* in my speech. You can see why I got beat up a lot in high school.

I decide to include this poem in *THE BREAD IS IN THE BED*, but that I would only bore the reader with the first stanza. I will print the complete poem as an addendum. It occurs to me that I should include it in *this* book as well. It's suitable advice for both *authors and innkeepers!* Make it so, Mr. Worf (a little *Star Trek Next Gen* reference there).

The cynic in me is saying that I only cut-and-pasted this poem to get another easy page sardined into a pathetic page count. (Shut up, cynic in me.)

Now that Ann and her mom's schedules have freed up, their JetBlue flight to Florida has them arriving in six days. As much as I am eager to see and hug both of them, I think I have a better shot of completing this project while walking around an empty apartment and scratching my unshaven face. Authors aren't supposed to shave during writing projects, isn't that correct? I'm sure that I read that somewhere.

Ann asks if the video from last week's bluegrass jam (with me playing the ukulele and wearing the big gray beard) went up on YouTube. I tell her that I'll ask tomorrow and then I say, "umm, about that."

Thirty years of marriage is all you really need to convey an entire paragraph in three words. She says, "*Oh no, you're not!*" She instantly knows that I am growing a *real* beard, and in that same split second I know that I will be shaving it off before I pick her and her mother up at the airport. There will be no need for additional communication on this subject.

It's not that we don't have long discussions anymore; it's just that we've developed a kind of marital linguistic shorthand. I encourage you to do this in your relationship; it frees up more time for watching football.

5:45 PM – Although it's time for me to hop in the car and go to fishing class, I've decided to play hooky. Ann has been an idea machine lately, and I have four emails from her with notes to squeeze into the manuscript. If I am following the 21 Day plan, it all has to be written by midnight or I will turn into a pumpkin. The pile of index cards has a dent in it, but still looks menacing.

10:00 PM - It was quite the productive day today as you can see by the word count total. _THE BREAD IS IN THE BED_ flew past the blog and left it in her dust. I didn't quite get to the bottom of my note card pile, but I see the light at the end of the tunnel (and with any luck it's not an oncoming train). Tomorrow I will zip through the rest of my index cards, and then incorporate Ann's latest emails. It's interesting brainstorming with her from across the country. Usually we are in the same room. We have worked together since we bought the inn in 1986, and have been side-by-side 24/7 most of the time since. This is the longest time that we have been apart since my dad's 1995 heart surgery. Being apart for 21 days would have been a world record for us (by a full two weeks) and if I were to psychoanalyze myself it wouldn't be too much of a stretch to see why I decided to fill the time with a writing project like this.

I send in an online order to Dominos for a late night supper since I didn't have time to cook. A little window pops up that tells me that Jesus is making my pizza, and I decide to take this as a good sign.

11:30 PM - So I'm lying in bed with my printout and pen and I start to make *just a few corrections* to the hard copy. Nothing major, you know, just a few little items that I might want to remember. Yeah, right. You can guess how this goes. Three hours later every page looks like a Jackson Pollock masterpiece.

*THE BREAD IS IN THE BED* word count – 21,101
BOOK TWO word count – 13,994

## Day 10

10:15 AM - I'm beginning to settle into a morning routine. Although wake-up times are all over the map, the mornings have developed into a daily pattern. I've never been much of a morning person, so the routine seems to be helping. I wake up and stumble to the second bedroom to turn on the computer, then continue to the kitchen to start the coffee. Back to the bathroom for tooth brushing and over to the computer to open the programs that I'm using (Microsoft Word, Dragon and a Firefox browser). Then it's back to the kitchen to grab the coffee. Just doing laps around the apartment helps get the blood circulating, and I can finally take a moment to remove the toothpicks that have been tenting open my eyelids.

My slow start today is due primarily to last night's late-night editing activities. I printed out BREAD BED and took it to bed intending to glance over it as I drifted to sleep. It was an incredible relief to actually have hard copy in my hands. Being old school, I don't quite trust digital files. I tell myself that I shouldn't worry because I have two file copies here in Florida and one in the cloud (whatever the hell that is).

You may as well tell me that there's nothing to worry about when I have to go to the dentist. Kids today don't give it a second thought, but I'm from the dental chair torture generation that was scarred for life. I know dentists don't hurt anymore just like I know files don't get lost anymore (*especially with two backups*). Nevertheless, I breathe a sigh of relief when I've got the printout in my hot little hand (or when I'm high-tailing it out of the dental office).

I might not be able to type, but I'm getting pretty quick with the Dragon software "voice typing" and mouse combination. I really don't have the time to train the software to listen to me, but I'm faster using it when I need to type more than four words. I can imagine "real" authors out there chuckling at the neophyte. Maybe my next book should be "*How I Learned to Type in 21 days*" and it will have a companion piece about *writing the book about writing the book* on typing.

My $5 e-book cover was waiting for me in the inbox this morning. I understand that serious authors will spend hundreds of dollars (*and much more with the big guns*) to craft attractive, enticing book covers. It is the same with the *road appeal* of a country inn: you can't show off your interior unless you have a great exterior that attracts a customer to the front door.

It becomes instantly clear what kind of quality you get for a paltry five dollar investment. Sure, it's nice enough, but it looks like it was done on the cheap (umm, Einstein, it *was* done on the cheap). I wasn't exactly expecting Rembrandt, but I had been hoping for something to work with, like maybe the picture of a bed and a pile of cash on it. Instead, the cover is all text in a few different fonts and backgrounds.

Tomorrow I'll spend time with a *real cover designer* to try to get more of what I am envisioning. The book is looking promising (at least in my mind) and I'm beginning to see it appealing to a broader market than the few people who are actually out hunting for country inns. And since web pages can store bottomless information, I'll put this first cover image up on thebreadisinthebed.com so that anybody who is interested in what I am describing here can see it.

11:23 AM - Time to get back to BREAD BED. For some reason when I dictated that last line into the Dragon software, it heard "bread bed" as "read that," which made it read my words back to me in a robot-like computer voice. It was creepy and cool at the same time.

I have a productive afternoon before I head off to bluegrass class at 5:30. I'll hold judgment until the end of the project, but I think that it would be awfully difficult to accomplish this book project in 21 days if you worked only a couple of hours per day as the book suggests. I've been logging *long hours* at the desk; one hour in the morning and one hour in the evening just wouldn't cut it. Granted, I've been doing unapproved editing and refining (like a heroin addict, I can't help myself) which accounts for the fact that there is still a pile of index cards on the dining room table. I've been singing this tune for a couple of days, but *tomorrow* I intend to have everything, no matter how poorly written, off of the index cards and on to the Word file. It's either that or the methadone clinic.

<u>THE BREAD IS IN THE BED</u> word count – 27,445

BOOK TWO word count – 15,190

## Day 11 – Halfway Point

My *Rainman-like* math skills tell me that if I am to finish this book in 21 days, the halfway point occurs sometime today. I'm not certain how I should feel about that. If I was riding a bell curve, I suppose that I would be at the very top of the graph about to roll down the other side and go screaming into the finish line.

As of now, I don't feel like I am building up huge momentum for the big finishing sprint. I may consider the screaming part, though. I know that it's a process, and that my thinking may change in another week, but I wanted to put these thoughts on the Day 11 page so I can look back to understand my precise mindset. So, Day 11 at 10:53 AM is a big "no" to *confidence* and "yes" to *screaming*.

With the attention span of a gnat, my thoughts drift back to the covers of these books. Now that I have decided to spend real money (defined as *more than $5*) on cover design, I contact my old fraternity brother John. He designed the poster for my college senior thesis lecture: *Adaptations of Aquatic Animals to Lakes and Ponds*; subtitle: *Water Bugs and Other Neat Stuff!* It was a very funny cartoon of a bunch of bugs sitting in an auditorium listening to a speaker (a caricature of me) lecturing behind a podium.

John is now a successful cartoonist for a large Pennsylvania newspaper. It's just bad timing that we have only recently had some political differences. As a Libertarian, I seem to piss everyone off at one time or another. I am socially liberal and fiscally conservative, which is a political square peg that doesn't get pounded easily into today's partisan round holes. While John and I agree on most social issues, we have recently had a difference of opinion on other matters (on Facebook, of course).

But a 37-year-old friendship takes precedence over a recent squabble, and I send him a note explaining what I am doing and asking if he can help. I want to "remember the little people" that rocket me to stardom. Plus, he's a damn funny guy.

I also take a moment to contact "Luiz the Computer Guy" to get on his schedule. I would like to have a webpage and Facebook page for these books by the time they are uploaded. I understand from both Lisa's publishing class and John Locke's *How to sell* book that getting "Liked" on Facebook is much more than an ego boost - it can lead to increased sales.

Luiz is one of those "high-schoolers" that we advise you to rent in BREAD BED. His successful high school career has grown into a computer help business, and now that he has graduated he's doing quite well for himself. This is the entrepreneurial spirit that we're trying to foster in the innkeeping book.

While chatting into the microphone I glance over and see the headset that came with the Dragon software. I am not using the Dragon headset; I am using the Alienware headset that I purchased with my laptop. It is 100 times more comfortable than the clip-on Dragon headset, but even the nice one is starting to bother me. Maybe if I were killing bad guys in *Diablo III* it wouldn't be noticeable, but now that I'm trying to concentrate on sentence structure I am much more aware of it. Maybe before my next book I'll find the Rolls-Royce of headsets.

It's dinner time and I'm *still struggling* to turn the index cards into paragraphs. I can't seem to bring myself to just write them into the manuscript and find a home for them later. I'm trying to find the exact spot where they belong and this is getting increasingly difficult. It's probably because I didn't stick to the outline and my organization sucks. I'm going to slam on the brakes and organize a Table of Contents. Then I'll cut the sections like a Ginsu knife commercial and paste them where they belong. I've skipped Photoshop class tonight because I'm feeling the pressure of falling behind on the writing. This should be Day 1 of the *second* draft and I'm still writing the *first* draft. Arrrgh.

Reading the above, I realize that my funny bone has gone on hiatus. I think I'll take Steve Martin's advice and "*Put a slice of baloney in each shoe.*" That way I'll "*Feel funny.*"

1:36 AM - I've been at this all day, and I feel a little better, though I don't feel as wonderful as I had envisioned. I've got a reasonable handle on the chapters and have condensed them into two parts and eight chapters. It's a little strange knowing that our innkeeping book is somewhat opinionated, and that a lot of people in the innkeeping world won't exactly be thrilled by our publication. On the other hand, it's a tiny ripple in a tiny pond, so what's the big deal? Maybe next time I'll stick to something less controversial (then again, that might be *boring*).

*THE BREAD IS IN THE BED* word count – 31,646
BOOK TWO word count – 16,356

## Day 12

My drift-off-to-sleep book last night was _Building Your Book for Kindle_ by Amazon. It explained the formatting conventions that I _should have been following_ all along. I'll have to go back and make corrections to both manuscripts, and even though it's not the end of the world, I'm beginning to grasp why many writers are neurotic. I've been bouncing from one anxiety to the other these last two weeks (OK, 12 days, but who's counting? Oh right, me.)

I know that we've got something interesting to say, but then I worry if we will tell it well enough. Earlier I was worried that the book wouldn't be long enough and that buyers would feel cheated. Now that I've done the word-count math, I'm happy with the length but I wonder if it will be funny enough? Jokes that were making me laugh out loud the first time around now seem only mildly humorous because I've proof read them repeatedly. How many times can that chicken cross the road?

Intuitively I know that these are simply first-time author growing pains. As with innkeeping, the nuts and bolts of the work will soon become second nature. It's no wonder authors buy Maalox by the pallet load. I've heard them gripe about the writing process, but I have never quite understood it until now.

So I'm reading the design and formatting advice in my latest e-book, which tells me exactly how to format the Front Matter (title page, copyright, dedication, table of contents, and preface *or* introduction) and the Back Matter (end notes, glossary, for further reading/bibliography, index). Somewhere in between is your *actual book*, and this is referred to as the Doesn't Matter.

It's always struck me that the Dedication in the beginning of books (pardon me, in the *Front Matter*) was kind of awkward. When you dedicate something, aren't you supposed to be doing something in advance, such as "I shall henceforth dedicate my life to ensuring the survival of the left-handed spotted owl?"

I read through a few Dedications, and they seem to be either "thank you's" or "suck ups." I'd like to thank my wonderful family for staying out of my hair and not putting cyanide in my coffee because I've been such an ass lately. Or I'd like to thank all the wonderful people out there (and you know who you are) that inspired *me* to pen this self-sacrificing work of art.

Other than authors, who dedicates any work *that they've already done* to someone? Even ribbon cutters are dedicating *someone else's* work. I can imagine my breakfast conversation with Ann when I tell her that I have worked incredibly hard these past three weeks, I would like to dedicate them to her. "Thank you honey; would you please pass the sugar?" Or Joe Six Pack saying to Mrs. Pack, "I'm off to another shift on the factory floor. But first I want you to know that I'm dedicating my previous month on the job to you." *"For all you do, this Bud's for you."*

Book dedications were here long before the internet, which finally gave us the ability to tell people how much we care about them without actually having to speak with them. Today if I want to tell a relative that she is important in my life, I can forward something meaningful to her (and nine other friends).

Here's a wild thought: if you want to tell your wife that you love her, maybe you could open the door and mention it? Putting these sentiments in a Dedication is the author's equivalent of jumping up and down on Oprah's couch like Tom Cruise; it seems a little self-serving. So here I am, two weeks into my writing career and already pissing off my co-workers. That reminds me that it's time to get back to BREAD BED so I can tick off some innkeepers.

11:22 AM - It seems that it was only yesterday that I was at the halfway point of the project. Oh right, it *was* only yesterday. Now I have the more intimidating way to say it: *I only have nine days left!* If I were wearing boots now, I would be quaking inside them.

The ears on my bunny slippers, however, are only trembling slightly.

7:25 PM - As I'm logging my 12th complete day in a row, I can't help but think that Steve's book was a *tad optimistic*. I was supposed to be able to produce this book in my spare time, working an hour in the morning and an hour at night. I suppose if I were writing *"How to Disassemble a Toilet,"* I could do it in that time frame. (Lord knows, I've taken apart enough toilets in my illustrious career.) But since I'm trying to distill fifteen years of innkeeping into cogent advice, all the while reliving war stories, it's taking slightly longer. The toilet book is sounding pretty good now.

I learned in *Building Your Book for Kindle* that my book needs to be specifically formatted so that when I upload it the software can generate a functional Table of Contents. As I'm following through the formatting guide, I realized that my starter version of Microsoft Word does not have the Table of Contents auto-formatting feature.

So it's off to the internet to get the latest version of Word, and I learn that I can get a free 30-day trial. If it's free, it's for me. The only problem is the Microsoft account team is having a *"temporary problem"* and won't let me log on to my newly created account. They're polite enough to ask me to "Please try again later," but it's been a few hours of "later" and it's starting to annoy me. Apparently we have a different understanding of the word "temporary."

I'm going to bed, where I can get 8-hours of *temporary* sleep…

*THE BREAD IS IN THE BED* word count – 33,421
BOOK TWO word count – 17,357

## Day 13

I stayed in bed until noon today. It's not that I was completely bushed (well maybe a little) but that I was horizontal with last night's printout.

BREAD BED is starting to look like a real book, particularly in the first 25 pages. The last 40 or so are a little haphazard, so I thought I would try to tidy them up on paper instead of on the laptop. This led to a brief conversation with myself, in which I was convinced that I should really be doing this work from the comfort of my pillow.

I checked my email before I began to make these corrections on the Word file and learned that Ann's flight to Florida tomorrow has been canceled. Rats. Winter storm Nemo has thrown a wrench into the JetBlue operation, and even though the runways will be cleared, the Boston roads are expected to be impassable. The short of it is I don't get to see the girls until Thursday (Day 18).

At least my fledgling beard has been given a reprieve for a few days. I had planned to give Ann the old George Carlin line, "Honey, I've always *had* a beard; I just grew it on the *inside*," but that strategy had "fizzle" written all over it. I'll also have to remind her to bring down the snow shovel so I can clean up 2 ½ weeks' worth of bachelor pad.

Don't you just love it how they name *every snowstorm* now to increase the drama? It's not the National Weather Service doing the storm naming; it's *a TV station!* And the "news" networks report The Weather Channel's storm names as if they were gospel. (You lie, and I'll swear to it!)

Up until recently, the weather was pretty boring programming unless a storm with a name was smashing into a coastline somewhere. Now we have our crack action weather teams reporting curbside: *"This just in Chet: two snowflakes exactly alike have been sighted in Somerville; back to you in the studio!"*

Why not take a good thing and run with it? Someone at the Weather Channel must've said, *"Hey, let's start naming winter storms so we can get more people to tune into our show!"* So this year they started giving quirky names to storms, including Nemo, Gandalf, Herpes and Khan (as in *Star Trek, Wrath of*).

Next year maybe they'll start naming traffic jams. They could put eye-in-the-sky traffic reporters in gunship helicopters. I'd tune in for that. (I'm picturing Les Nessman from *WKRP in Cincinnati* in full combat regalia looking like Michael Dukakis popping out of a Sherman tank, but then again I'm pretty old and I remember that crap.)

It's Saturday evening and Microsoft is into the second day of their "temporary problem." I'm going to have to find another way to get a better Word program. (When you go the cheap route it's easy to get hoisted on your own petard, and mine is beginning to hurt.) The annoying thing is Bing keeps grabbing my browser every time I try to search and it redirects me to the Microsoft login page, which alerts me (yet again) of the *"temporary problem."* Help! The Software Overlords are sinking their hooks into me.

10:57 PM - It takes until now to put all of my notes into the manuscript (and I've been at it since lunch). I did some rewriting and paragraph crafting, all those things that real authors do at this stage. A long dormant feeling surfaces as I think, *"I'm done!"* Of course I'm not really finished, but at this point it's reached the "good enough" stage that would have satisfied me back in high school. (Hey, I said it was *long dormant.*)

Oh, and by the way, the Weather Channel didn't actually name the winter storm "Herpes," they named it Xerxes, which sounds just as gross.

*THE BREAD IS IN THE BED* word count – 33,477
BOOK TWO word count – 18,251

## Day 14

Just when I thought that I could predict what to expect in my writing day, I am surprised again. I thought that after I took all that time yesterday to incorporate my notes into the manuscript, today's review would require a lot less ink. That is absolutely not the case as I'm finding it necessary to continue to rework paragraphs. Most of the typos are gone but it is now midafternoon and I have only re-worked half of the book. I would say that I'm hopeful tomorrow's work will require less ink, but my confidence in that is crumbling.

In the frigid Northeast, as expected, JetBlue resumed service today. It's too bad that they jumped the gun and canceled Ann's flight. Once that happens, everybody is kicked off of the manifest and must fend for themselves rebooking later flights. After hours of trying, Ann and her mom finally get another flight, and they'll be here the day after tomorrow (Day 16).

9:32 PM – Lord love a duck, it's taken until now to make all of my corrections. There is no way on this green earth that I could have done this "in my spare time" as Steve suggested. Of course I *knew* it couldn't be done with an hour in the morning and an hour in the evening; I'm just poking fun. Kind of.

I have my editing team on standby: Steve 1 and Steve 2. Steve 1 is a brainiac fraternity brother and former editor of our college newspaper; Steve 2, my humor editor, is my cousin who is burdened with an enlarged funny bone. So as you can see, between the 21 Days guy and my two editors, I'm rotten with Steves, and you can feel free to blame any of them for the deficiencies in this book.

*THE BREAD IS IN THE BED* word count – 33,121
BOOK TWO word count – 18,536

## Day 15

Since BREAD BED is looking mostly like a book, I decided to do a little housekeeping today and fight the good fight with Microsoft. No luck since the "temporary" problem is still happening. I cut and paste the error message into Google, and discover that I'm not the first person to have this challenge. The frustrations of other people ooze out of the many discussion threads. Others have been pulling their hair out since June, so my brain finally gets the memo and decides to find another source for the new software.

That's enough of this noise, so I go off to Dell to purchase Microsoft Word from them. Everything goes swimmingly, and I get an activation code. When I click the download link to put in this code I am *sent to the Microsoft page with the temporary problem*. I am stunned, amazed, and deflated all at the same time. It's like hiking a mountain and rounding that last bend when you think you're at the top, and seeing another hill going straight up. You just want to toss your pack down on the ground and put your head in your hands.

I send a halfhearted request to Dell for help, but how are they really going to help with the Microsoft page? I'm hoping that they can send me the software by another method, and I'm also hoping that the Red Sox go undefeated this year.

I'll try to pick up a copy of Word from Best Buy tonight on my way to publications class.

The really cool news of the day, of interest to any author, is a web page that I found called paperrater.com. If you cut-and-paste your manuscript onto the site, it evaluates your paper for spelling, grammar, word choice, style and vocabulary. It even gives you a grade, and though it is quick to tell you that it can't guarantee that your thoughts make any sense, at least you wrote them in a grammatically correct manner.

I'm heartened that my paper gets an "A," so at least I know that even if it's mental gibberish, at least I've conveyed it in proper English. I make the suggested corrections (including the few typos that had escaped my notice) and resubmit hoping for an "A+." My brown nosing does not pay off; maybe I should have uploaded a digital apple.

Dell software support sends me a note suggesting that I try to download my new Word program using the Microsoft Internet Explorer browser. I do this and it works immediately. What an *incredible coincidence* that I'm unable to download a Microsoft product without using the Microsoft browser. I yield to the Software Overlords.

Unfortunately, my new and improved Word program seems to want to refresh every three to five seconds, and the entire screen blinks and flashes in an incredibly annoying pattern. If I were subject to seizures, I would be on the floor doing the horizontal mambo about now.

*THE BREAD IS IN THE BED* word count – 33,150
BOOK TWO word count – 19,438

## Day 16

I breathed a huge sigh of relief this morning when John says that he will be able to work up cover art before Monday. I give him my rough idea of what I want, but trust him completely as he is the professional. And anyway, he had me at *Water Bugs and Other Neat Stuff.*

While my Word screen is flashing like a 1970's disco, I'm marveling at the organizational ability of the automatic Table of Contents. This would have saved a lot of time if I had been using it all along, but still will make the final organizing much easier.

1:00 PM - Ann and her mom arrive this afternoon, sneaking out of Boston just before the next snowstorm arrives. I'm planning to pick her up at the airport wearing my Party Store gray beard from bluegrass night. Underneath will be *my own unshaven mug* that she won't see until I remove the gag beard. We Stanford's really know how to milk a joke.

This reminds me of the year that I bought Ann's Christmas presents at the Disney Store. I am a huge fan, and I got her Mickey Mouse sweaters, hats, shirts and about anything else that they would sell me. Then I went down to the other end of the mall to buy gift boxes from Victoria's Secret. When we had *family Christmas present opening*, she was in full-panic mode while everybody watched her open her gifts. Of course, it wasn't till later that evening when we were alone that I gave her the Disney-boxed gift...

4:00 PM - I get Ann home from the airport and want to show her how much I have missed her these past two weeks, so we race to the bedroom.

4:02 PM - Wow, that was great! I'm newly inspired to get back to the writing. But first I have to shave.

Ann is concerned that I am being too personal with this book. She says that there are some things that should remain private. But this time I can't help myself. Maybe my next book should be a bodice ripper.

With my lovely bride and mother-in-law in the house, my freight train of progress grinds to a thundering halt. Lucky me, I get to go to the Naples Philharmonic for the ballet tonight. Who would not want to miss fishing class for that, anyway? I figure since our relationship survived another football season that I still owe her.

8:00 PM – Curtain rises.

11:00 PM – What can I say about the ballet?

11:01 PM – Back to the project. I send Smashwords an email for an auto return list of people (not associated with the company) able to properly format my Word files into *Smashword-ready Word files*. Smashwords runs the file through their Meatgrinder program which produces the (different) digital formats required for Kindle, iPad, Nook, Kobo and others. Think of it as taking a cow and processing it into a round burger for Burger King, a square one for Wendy's and a bunch of little tiny patties for your midnight White Castle run.

_THE BREAD IS IN THE BED_ word count – 33,064

BOOK TWO word count – 19,914

## Day 17

Book-wise it was a straightforward but boring day. It was read, correct, and repeat. All day long. At 5:30 PM we sent manuscripts to Steve 1 and Steve 2 and I went off to bluegrass class.

Bluegrass night was hilarious. The last two weeks when I got up to sing *Man of Constant Sorrow*, I was wearing my shaggy gray beard. Tonight when I got up to do my song (without the beard) a bunch of people pulled out gag hats and mustaches and put them on. There really is nothing like old-fashioned, good clean fun.

When I got back from class, Ann was mortified that we had emailed the manuscript because she had found another dozen "challenges" that will be caught by Steve 1 (and make us look like the amateurs we are). Well, it can't be helped, we have to keep moving this train down the tracks.

Quick story: when we drive from New Hampshire to Florida, we like to take the Amtrak Auto Train that leaves from northern Virginia in the late afternoon and arrives in the middle of Florida on the next morning. We can put in a good day driving, then load our car on the Auto Train and keep making progress, saving 900 miles of driving while we relax in the bar car. We sleep in a stateroom and arrive fresh the next morning for the final five-hour leg home.

What, you may ask, does this have to do with writing TWO e-books in 21 days? Well, I'll tell you! I sent an email to a Smashwords formatter in New Zealand asking him if he could put me on his schedule for this coming Monday. This will allow me to work all day Sunday and email my files to him at 8 PM Sunday night *my* time. Ten seconds later he will receive the files at 2 PM Monday afternoon *his* time. He can work on my formatting while I sleep Sunday night, and the Smashwords-ready files will be in my inbox when I wake up on *my* Monday morning. For the visual, picture me in all my cleverness, making a cunning face rubbing my hands together like a mad scientist.

Also, I figured out what is behind the discotheque blinking on my new Microsoft Word program: it is fighting with the Dragon program. I suspect that there is a techie answer to this, but I don't have the time to figure it out. I'm just glad that the bulk of the writing is over.

_THE BREAD IS IN THE BED_ word count – 32,586

BOOK TWO word count – 22,294

## Day 18

The punctuation parade continues as we are still finding typos and the occasional extra word in BREAD BED. I found an extra "that" in a paragraph I must have proof read a dozen times. Not only was it surprising to find such a blatant mistake, it was nerve racking because this word should have been edited out days ago. Granted, there are now groups of pages at a time that are completely bereft of editing scribble, but I'm still disappointed to stumble upon goofy errors.

Tomorrow will be the third day in a row of read, correct and repeat. I'll do a very slow read out loud to catch the last nasty mistakes that are still playing hide and seek.

I'm visiting with dad tomorrow morning, and it will be interesting to hand him the BREAD BED manuscript. He used to be a very talented writer and could turn quite the phrase. Now I'm not sure he can remember from one page to the next, but since he does live in the moment I expect that we'll get a few chuckles.

It was very exciting to see John's cover art today! He sent the rough drafts of both books, and they hit both nails on their respective heads. The BREAD BED cover looks both professional and whimsical. The font is businesslike but there's a cartoon character of an innkeeper sleeping soundly on a big bag of money. These are only the rough drafts, and he has yet to colorize them, but they look fantastic.

I got a quick text from Steve 1 who had a chuckle over some of the stories. I'm planning to incorporate his edits in the final two days.

My genius plan for Smashword formatting on the other side of the globe fell through. The New Zealand formatter was quite friendly and would have loved to do it, but is on vacation this week. I wrote to several other formatters on "Mark's List," and one of them agreed to block Monday off for me. I will send the Word files to her last thing Sunday night and she will be able to work on them Monday morning, returning them in the afternoon. Luiz will come over at dinner time to assist in the technical aspects of publishing.

We'll also put up the new webpage (thebreadisinthebed.com).

BREAD BED has been getting the most attention these last few days, and I'm going to have to do some serious catch-up editing of the manuscript for *this* book. I plan to do that while I'm visiting dad, and when I get back in the afternoon I'll incorporate the changes and send them to Steve 1.

It's now midnight, so I'm 72 hours from the self-imposed, completely arbitrary, cast-in-stone deadline. What could *possibly* go wrong?

*THE BREAD IS IN THE BED* word count – 32,594

BOOK TWO word count – 22,545

**Day 19**

I checked my email right before going to bed, and found Steve 1's edits. I stayed up till 3AM incorporating them into the manuscript and went to bed feeling *awesome*.

John emailed with last minute cover questions and said that he'd have the finals for me on Sunday. If you ever want to have a professional cartoonist help you with your project, I can't recommend John highly enough. He gives you every reason to keep pressing the "Like" button.

Proof, correct and repeat is becoming a mantra. We've almost memorized the manuscript. How do the typos keep hiding? What gremlins sneak in and jump on the keyboard in the middle of the night? Ann (and her mom) keep unearthing the little buggers. If I was felling trees to print this book I would be paranoid. But since I'm all digital (and can make corrections at will) I won't have to be fitted for my straight jacket yet.

Trials and tribulations on the formatting front: after my New Zealand Smashwords plan dissolved, the new Monday lady is also not going to work.

She sent me the invoice to be paid in advance. She would format the books for $85 dollars each, which sounded reasonable to me. Those on Mark's List that publish prices show a range of $40-100 for not-too-complicated manuscripts.

The problem is that while she was only going to charge me her standard fee for each manuscript, she wanted *$400 EXTRA* to schedule the work on Monday! It's not like she's pulling an all-nighter; she's just moving me up in her queue! She's not working any *harder* on my stuff, she is just getting to it sooner.

I was expecting maybe time-and-a-half or even slightly more (because it's President's Day), but triple time plus? Thanks, but no thanks. I can make a lot of mistakes for $400 and have a much better time making them!

I had a very enjoyable time writing the ending to this book today (so I cheated, sue me.) It was a reality check that the project is coming to an end even though it doesn't seem so with all the work that is still ahead.

_THE BREAD IS IN THE BED_ word count – 32,504

BOOK TWO word count – 22,500

## Day 20

The unpublished verse from the musical *Annie* started, *"The book'll be done, tomorrow! Bet your bottom dollar that tomorrow, you'll be done!"*

We're down to the short strokes and I haven't heard from Steve 2 yet. Maybe he's doubled over laughing and can't find the keyboard to send back his humor suggestions. You can't rush funny.

The book corrections are dry and tiring. I feel like a Bedouin stumbling toward a desert mirage looking for water. Read…correct…repeat…

*THE BREAD IS IN THE BED* word count – 32,676
BOOK TWO word count – 19,464

## Day 21 - Last Day

Wow! Is the last day really here? Where has the time flown?

The whole project is threatening to end *"not with a bang, but a whimper."* It's been a tedious "read, correct and repeat" for a few days now, and it's getting harder to concentrate. If I haven't caught a typo by now, it's not going to be found by me.

4:47 PM - John's finished covers arrive in my inbox. They look fantastic! I am re-energized to try to make the insides live up to the cover art, so I print out the latest copy of each book and go lie down to read and correct - *one final time!*

6:24 PM - Steve 1's edits of *this book* come back, and I take some time to incorporate them into the manuscript. I get a real-life LOL when he suggests that I put in arbitrary time stamps instead of rounding to the nearest 30 minutes. It was only funny because I just did the time rounding yesterday before I sent him the manuscript. I was thinking that the precise time stamps looked a little anal retentive, so I rounded them (all except Day 4, which was *too funny* with the meticulous times). It only takes me about 10 minutes to put back the original time stamps. So yes, dear reader, the times in the book are accurate IRL (that's "In Real Life," nana).

9:00 PM – Let's see, do I watch the Downton Abbey Season Finale or do I honor my pledge to finish these books before midnight? Integrity wins and I hit the cable box record button and head to my room to type while Ann and her mom watch TV.

You might ask, *"Other than three weeks of your life that you will never get back, how much did this cost out of pocket? Please do not include pizza expenses."*

The total investment for publishing *TWO* eBooks came to...drum roll... $683.76.

See what I mean about a whimper?

Here's my expense breakdown:
Steve Smith, *How to Write a Nonfiction eBook in 21 days* - $2.99

John Locke, *How I Sold 1 Million eBooks in 5 Months* - $2.99

thebreadisinthebed.com domain for one year - $1

Two reams of paper - $12.38

Two black ink cartridges - $38.42

Dragon talk-to-type software - $50.99

Fiverr.com cover fail - $5

Microsoft Word - $79.99

Index cards (had 'em) - $0

Cover Art - (each $120) - $240*

Smashwords formatting - $0

ISBN Number - (each $125) - $250**

Tax, Title and Dealer Prep - $0

*It wouldn't be fair to John, so I didn't print the actual price that I paid for his covers. He does incredible work, but unless you were his fraternity brother over 30 years ago I doubt that you have any good blackmail stories that can help you whittle down his price. I estimated $120 per book, which I understand is the cost of a reasonably good cover. Clearly I came out way ahead in this category. If you want John's freelance assistance, inquiries regarding his illustration and cartoon work can be made via h20vale@msn.com.

**The ISBN numbers at Bowker.com are $125 each, but if you give them $250 then you get 10 numbers. Watch out world, I have 8 more ISBN numbers looking for a home!

By my calculations (*"Hey, they said that there wouldn't be math"*) I'm looking to break even sometime between now and the next time Sylvester Stallone has a hit movie.

## Final Thoughts

At the beginning of this book I said that I would try to tackle a few questions: What's it like to write your first e-book? Is it difficult? Can I do it? (And why is there air?)

I spent the last 21 days, ad nauseam, detailing the answer to the first question of what it's like to write your first e-book. It's comparable to a wild roller coaster ride where you never hold on to the safety bar because you have both hands in the air for the whole trip. In one hand you are balancing a delicious extra-large Brooklyn-style pizza, say half-mushroom and half-pepperoni (representing your everyday family and social life). In the other hand you are holding a 64oz mug filled to the rim with quadruple Vente triple-shot espresso, half-vanilla extra whip (representing your writing project). Your goal is to enjoy the ride, enjoy the meal, and enjoy a soothing beverage before you arrive at the end jubilant and spotless.

Good luck with that, sport. Jubilant, yes. It's an incredible feeling to write the words *"The End"* after all the hard work. Spotless, no. I feel like I'm drenched in java and have pepperoni stuck in my hair. *I love it!*

Is it difficult? Hell, yes. For me, anyway. You may have more gray matter with which to work. Most of *my* gray matter is on the *outside* of my head.

Can you do it? Again, hell yes! E-Publishing is easy. The bar is very low; all it takes is a modicum of computer savvy. Whether anybody *likes* your book is a whole other conversation!

I believe that everyone has something interesting to say. Whether you say it well is another story. *"Stay in school, kids."* Also, *"Give a hoot, don't pollute."* Your book may suck, but it won't be the last one to do so. If you're afraid of ridicule, then I suggest ukulele lessons. That ought to toughen you up.

As to the last question, why is there air? To blow up footballs, of course!

## The End

Wow, was *that* fun to write. I'm gonna do it again.

The End

(Really, this time.)

## Acknowledgements

I could not have written this book without Jesus, who was there for me in my time of need. He makes the absolute best Brooklyn-style pizza in Florida, and some nights I just did not have the time to cook. He even made the one that was ½ pepperoni and ½ mushrooms. With him all things are possible. Also, thanks to Pedro for delivering them to my door.

Thank you Steve Scott for your book *How to Write a Nonfiction eBook in 21 days*. Without your arbitrary deadlines that I stuck to like glue, it might have taken me 22 days.

Thank you John Locke for your marketing advice in *How I Sold 1 Million eBooks in 5 Months*. If I could capture just a fraction of your devoted following, I'd be a happy man. Well, I suppose that I *will* capture a fraction, albeit a microscopic one.

Thanks to Will the Comcast guy and Richard the painter. Without your assistance, I could probably have written them in 20 days.

Next to last and definitely least, Steve 1. Friends may come and friends may go…..you've been a friend through thick and thin.

And to Annster, love of my lions.

## Addendum – Don't Quit

### DON'T QUIT

When things go wrong, as they sometimes will,

When the road you're trudging seems all uphill,

When the funds are low and the debts are high,

And you want to smile, but you have to sigh,

When care is pressing you down a bit,

Rest, if you must, but don't you quit.


Life is queer with its twists and turns,

As every one of us sometimes learns,

And many a failure turns about,

When he might have won had he stuck it out;

Don't give up though the pace seems slow -

You may succeed with another blow.


Often the goal is nearer than,

It seems to a faint and faltering man,

Often the struggler has given up,

When he might have captured the victor's cup,

And he learned too late when the night came down,

How close he was to the golden crown.

Success is failure turned inside out –

The silver tint of the clouds of doubt,

And you never can tell how close you are,

It may be near when it seems so far,

So stick to the fight when you're hardest hit –

It's when things seem worst that you mustn't quit.


-Author unknown

**A preview of <u>The Bread is in The Bed</u>:**

THE
# BREAD
IS IN THE
# BED

MORE
*How to Make Money*
*as a B&B Innkeeper*

By Glen and
Ann Stanford

This book is the layered onion of e-books, but less stinky.

On the outside it's a humor book that will bring tears to your eyes; and inside of that it's a business book; and inside of that is some sage advice on customer service; and deep down inside of that is the one-of-a-kind advice specifically tailored to the innkeeper on how to make money today, tomorrow, and in the years happily ever after.

YES! There is a way to make money as an innkeeper! This book cuts to the most important aspect of innkeeping: profit! What? Isn't the lifestyle the most important? Isn't it the joy of owning your own business? Isn't it the pride in one's soul that can only be achieved with a clean, shining toilet?

Maybe so, but if you don't have the money to keep your dream going, you'll never get a chance to take pleasure in your new career. This book addresses (what should be) your biggest fear: "How do I get money into the cash register?" You can work on your fear of napkin folding on your own time.

*THE BREAD IS IN THE BED* might not be a humor book in the strictest sense. It's more the literary equivalent of a genetic love child from Leona Helmsley, Dave Barry, Dale Carnegie and Donald Trump. You'll learn valuable secrets to making (more) money in the innkeeping business, all the while keeping your sense of humor, winning friends, influencing people, and maintaining epic hair. It's a funny book, it's a business book, it's got unique innkeeper advice, it's a breath mint and it's a candy mint!

"Ah ha," you say, "Jack of all trades, master of none." Guilty as charged. But let's modify that expression to "Jack of all trades and decidedly good advice on one – the innkeeping money stuff!" And despite all the discussion about the innkeeper's cash register, this is a fun book that will make you smile, *particularly* if you have no intention of ever owning an inn!

Nowadays, entrepreneurship is the widest highway to financial success. There is risk and reward in every job, but you only have so much time to devote to your occupation. If you want to quit the rat race and run your own rats, you need to become an entrepreneur. If you want your inn, B&B or guesthouse to actually make money, this could be a pretty important book in your arsenal. After 27 years (and counting) as entrepreneurs, we believe that running your own business is the surest way for most people to maximize the reward of their efforts. We're going to help you find the best location for your new property, giving you some useful advice before it's too late. Then we'll talk about how an attitude adjustment can lead to increased profits.

Sure, it can be scary to strike out on your own. Maybe that is why innkeeping attracted me in the first place. I knew that I already had many of the skills required to keep an inn. I could flip a pancake, make a bed (occasionally) and pour a beer (more than occasionally). What else did I need to know? Ahh, the ignorance of bliss, I remember it well.

(One odd convention you will encounter throughout the book is the switching between first-person singular and first-person plural. When you encounter the word "I" it means that Glen is telling a story and trying to be funny, and Ann has disavowed all knowledge, like the recording at the beginning of every *Mission Impossible* episode. So, I'm the "I" and Ann and I are the royal "we." Why am "I" not surprised?)

We're going to tell the innkeepers out there how to make more money starting today! And we really mean *today* (if you have guests in the inn tonight, that is.) Then we're going to tell you the things that you can do to make more money *this month*. And then, most importantly, we will outline the strategies that you can begin to use starting immediately that will improve your profitability *this year* and in *every year* to come.

There's a big hint on how you are going to do this right on the cover of this book: the bread is in the bed! The money is in the mattress! The profit is in the pillows! You won't be making your big profits by selling golf shirts, souvenirs, or even meals and drinks. Your laser focus will be, must be, putting heads on the pillows.

*Running a Bed and Breakfast for Dummies* by Mary White is a tremendous compilation for *every detail* you might need to consider before purchasing a hospitality property, and we highly recommend it. For better or worse, our book is *much* more streamlined and opinionated (and the humor is spicier!) We're going to tell you the best ways that *we* have found to succeed in this business, and 15 years of pancake flipping and bathroom cleaning confers a certain amount of street cred.

You might as well go get a whole bucket of asterisks because there are many ways to skin the innkeeping cat, and you will likely take issue with some of our opinions. The smart reader will understand that we don't mean to sound like know-it-alls, but we do have some interesting things to say. Then again, if you were smart, you wouldn't be getting into the innkeeping business, now would you?

Think of us as little imps sitting on your shoulder as you are reading the traditional "How to be an innkeeper" type book, smacking you upside the head and saying "pay attention here, this is important, this is the good stuff."

Once you buy your inn, you are automatically enrolled in the school of hard knocks. It is our intention to help you earn enough money to pay your tuition and graduate. We genuinely believe in what we're trying to convey: Innkeepers can absolutely make more money without having to go through (too much of) the painful learning curve.

The last section of this book is "War Stories from Innkeeping Hell." Most are comical, some are incredible, and most of them should help to talk you out of ever buying a country inn!

You'll find some stories that illustrate why you need to have an emergency fund for a rainy day. We will talk about where you should spend money and when you should keep it in your pocket. You've got to, as Kenny Rogers sings, *"Know when to hold 'em, know when to fold 'em."* Bruce, who runs the Inn at Water's Edge in Ludlow, Vermont with his lovely wife Tina, once gave me this excellent advice: "never trade with scared money." I told him that all my money is petrified, thank you very much. You will need an emergency fund for the unexpected things that seem to happen only to innkeepers (what's up with *that*, anyway?) Let's say - to choose an illustration completely out of thin air - that a deer jumps through your back window and rampages through your downstairs. Yes, that happened to us (and more on this incident later). I looked everywhere in the budget for "deer rampages" but couldn't find a thing.